PA-KUA: Eight-Trigram Boxing

CHINESE MARTIAL ARTS LIBRARY

PA-KUA
Eight-Trigram Boxing

Robert W. Smith
and Allen Pittman

TUTTLE PUBLISHING
Boston • Rutland, Vermont • Tokyo

Contents

Preface

We wrote this book believing that there are many people who are interested in the Chinese internal martial art of Pa-kua (pronounced "ba-gwa") as it was traditionally taught on the mainland.* Such people understand that this art is a meditative form of health and body management from which self defense spills over, rather than an aggressive combat form, of which the world already has too many. As a system of self defense, however, it is harshly effective.

Besides training for several years in Taiwan under the Pa-kua masters Hung I-hsiang and his brother Hung I-mien, Mr. Smith was also fortunate enough to be allowed to study under Wang Shu-chin, Kuo Feng-ch'ih, Yuan Tao, and other masters. His training path is very clearly outlined in his *Chinese Boxing: Masters and Methods* (Tokyo, 1974) and other books. Some twenty years later, Mr. Pittman, one of Mr. Smith's senior students, went to Taiwan seeking the old masters, but found that many had died. In Taipei, however, he came across a still hardy Hung I-mien, who invited him to share his home as a live-in student. After absorbing Hung's Hsing-i and Pa-kua, he traveled south to Taichung to practice with the sons of the late Ch'en P'an-

---

*In this book, Chinese terms are transliterated with the Wade-Giles system, except where the word is already widely used with a different spelling, as, for instance, "Peking, "Nanking," etc.

ling—Yuan-ch'ao and Yun-ch'ing—and the senior students of the late Wang Shu-chin.

From these experiences, the basic forms of these two master teachers as taught to the authors were assimilated and consolidated. This is the first time that they have been taught to the West in such minute detail. We hope that Western students will benefit from this exposition of teachings that were once only passed on to initiates deemed worthy of learning the styles and being entrusted with their transmission.

The Pa-kua forms given in this book are essentially those of Wang Shu-chin as elaborated in his *Pa-kua lien-huan chang* [Pa-kua Linked Palm] (Taipei, 1978; privately published). Also used as sources were the two books considered to be the best ever written on the art: Sun Lu-tang's classic *Pa-kua ch'uan hsueh* [A Study of Pa-kua Boxing] (Peking, 1916) and Huang Po-nien's *Lung-hsing pa-kua chang* [Dragon-Style Pa-kua Palm] (Shanghai, 1936). These are the orthodox, traditional methods long practiced on the mainland and in Taiwan—the authentic forms from which most other versions derive. They are being published here so that students can learn the *real* forms as opposed to the Americanized offshoots. These forms are designed to refine your nature, reform your temperament, and return you to your original self.

But it is a rash reader who thinks that by simply buying this book he or she will mysteriously be enabled to absorb the teachings it contains. To learn any of the three internal arts—Tai-chi, Hsing-i, or Pa-kua—requires commitment, not mere involvement. Being involved or committed is like ham and eggs: the chicken is involved but the pig is committed! This is not a coffee-table book—it should be sweat over and on. We have labored over its presentation, carefully blending the pictorial with the textual, so that the student can study correctly. But our efforts are in vain if the student does not practice. He or she must practice assiduously for a long time if progress is to come. Confucius once said that if he gave a student one corner of a handkerchief, it was up to the student to find the other three corners. This book is but one corner; your practice will help you find the other three.

Acknowledgments

The writing of this book was eased by the help and support of several friends and colleagues: John Lang, who diligently worked at every level of its preparation; James Klebau, a true professional, who caught the inner spirit of the forms in his fine photographs; Pat Kenny, who helped with the graphics; Bob Arief, Al Carson, Jay Falleson, Steve Goodson, and Irene Pittman, who proofread and corrected the manuscript; Y. W. Chang, Ann Carruthers, Pat McGowan, Chris Bates, Richard Cress, Danny Emerick, and Ben Lo, who acted as sounding-boards; Anne Pavay and Alice Smith, who patiently typed the manuscript; Stephen Comee, who studies under Wang Shu-chin's successor and who worked hard as the editor and designer of this book; the Charles E. Tuttle Company, which agreed to publish this book; and all the masters and teachers of the Chinese internal martial arts who have given their time and instruction—without their generosity we would never have been able to study these arts. To all of these and to others who helped bring this project to fruition, the authors gratefully bow in deep thanks.

Robert W. Smith
Allen Pittman

Flat Rock, NC

PART ONE

Introduction
to Pa-kua Boxing

1
What Is Pa-kua?

She moved in circles,
and those circles moved. . . .

—T. Roethke
"I Knew a Woman"

PHILOSOPHY AND PRACTICE

Pa-kua, pronounced "ba-gwa," is one of the three martial arts that comprise the internal system (*nei-chia*) of Chinese boxing. The theory of Pa-kua, based on the *Book of Changes (I Ching)*, is difficult, but actualized as *Pa-kua chang* (Pa-kua Palm), a boxing-meditational exercise, it is even more difficult. Done to cultivate the *tao* (the way), the circling movements of Pa-kua both manifest Heaven and Earth and order and organize *yin* and *yang*. They follow the seasons and benefit man. When practicing Pa-kua, you walk the circle as though macrocosmically walking in the universe, affecting and being affected microcosmically by the changes inside your body.

The name as well as the rationale of Pa-kua derive from the system of philosophy that gave rise to the *Book of Changes*—an ancient metaphysical treatise over three thousand years old but timeless in its wisdom. Originally a manual of oracles, the *Book of Changes* evolved into a compilation of ethical enumerations, eventually becoming such a compendium of knowledge that it was chosen as one of the Five

Classics of Confucianism. It became a common source for both Confucian and Taoist philosophy. The central theme of the book, as well as of the system of boxing, is that everything is in flux. While the book's basic idea is the continuous process of change underlying all existence, Pa-kua has absorbed these ideas and transmuted them into a system of exercise and self-defense.

Originally, the *Book of Changes* contained a collection of linear signs meant to be used as oracles. In the most rudimentary sense, these oracles confined themselves to the answers "yes" and "no." Thus, "yes" was symbolized by a single unbroken *yang* line (———), and "no" by a single broken *yin* line (— —). Time brought a need for differentiation and amplification, which required additional lines. Thus, the eight trigrams (or units of three lines ☰) evolved, and at a later date these were further expanded to create the sixty-four hexagrams (or units of six lines ䷀). The Chinese word for such a combination of lines is *kua* (diagram). This, then, is the origin of the word Pa-kua—the eight trigrams.

The eight trigrams that form the basis of the *Book of Changes* are as follows:

Name	Attribute	Image	Part of Body
Ch'ien, Creative	Strong	Heaven	Head, heart
K'un, Receptive	Yielding	Earth	Spleen, stomach
Chen, Arousing	Movement	Thunder	Liver, throat
K'an, Abysmal	Dangerous	Water	Kidneys, ears
Ken, Stillness	Resting	Mountain	Back, hands/feet
Sun, Gentle	Penetrating	Wind	Intestines
Li, Clinging	Brilliance	Fire	Heart, spirit
Tui, Joyous	Joyful	Lake	Lungs, chest

In turn, these trigrams are often arranged in a circle around a T'ai-chi (Great Ultimate) symbol, the familiar diagram divided into *yin* and *yang* (Fig. 1). As the two *yin* and *yang* lines combine into groups of three, they gather at the eight directions to form the eight trigrams.

1. The Pa-kua Diagram

The sixty-four hexagrams evolved from the combinations of the eight trigrams being paired with one another. The theory behind this is explained in the *Book of Changes*, where the trigrams are also identified with the human body.

The diagram of the eight trigrams shown in Figure 1 is based upon the philosophy of the *Book of Changes*. The symbology is broad enough to embrace all things in Heaven and Earth, and narrow enough to represent the workings of the human body. It forms a path that can be followed both in cultivating the *tao* and in studying Pa-kua boxing. It also forms the essence of Pa-kua: "If you do not understand the philosophical theory expounded by the diagram, but only perform the movements of Pa-kua," Wang Shu-chin writes, "you will merely be doing calisthenics."

The basic eight trigrams from the *Book of Changes* are correlated with the fundamental eight Pa-kua forms as follows:

1. ☰ **Ch'ien,** the Creative principle, is associated with strength and the image of Heaven. We learn from Nature: Heaven is great because it moves without stopping. The SINGLE CHANGE OF PALM, similarly, is continuous and smooth and promotes blood circulation. Practiced incorrectly, it can hurt the heart.

2. ☲ **Li,** the Clinging principle, is brilliant and is associated with fire, which adheres to whatever it burns. To do the DOUBLE CHANGE OF PALM correctly, you should be internally soft and externally hard, like a snake wriggling into its hole. If done correctly, this form will help you to feel united with the universe.

3. ☳ **Chen,** the Arousing principle, incites movement and vibration and is associated with thunder. When practicing HAWK SOARS UP TO HEAVEN, keep your upper body soft and lower body hard, externally quiet yet internally moving. Though still, you have the potential to move, and your enemy will be misled by your seeming lack of movement. Physically, the *ch'i* of your liver will be harmonized rather than agitated if you perform this form correctly.

4. ☷ **K'un,** the Receptive principle, is associated with yielding and with the Earth. YELLOW DRAGON ROLLS OVER stresses the unity of the upper and lower body, of the internal and the external. Practiced correctly, this form will make your body feel as light and agile as that of a fine horse.

5. ☵ **K'an,** the Abysmal principle, is associated with danger and with water. It indicates that in the midst of trouble you must persevere with self-confidence, which will lead to success. WHITE SNAKE STICKS OUT TONGUE stresses an appearance of softness but with a strong inner core: a strong mind and a soft hand movement. Practiced correctly, the form will help you to feel calm and centered, and will keep you from becoming dizzy.

6. ☶ **Ken,** the Stillness principle, represents the state of rest and is associated with mountains. When a bowl rests upside down, you cannot see what is in it. GIANT ROC SPREADS WINGS shows a tendency to be motionless. Practiced correctly, it will reduce the fire in your heart and enable your *ch'i* to reach the four extremities.

7. ☱ **Tui,** the Joyous principle, is associated with lowness and with lakes. In doing WHITE MONKEY PRESENTS A PEACH, keep your upper body soft and your middle and lower parts hard. Lower your body like a tiger squatting, prepared to pounce. Practiced correctly, this form will help your lungs to feel clear and will keep you from panting.

8. ☴ **Sun,** the Gentle principle, is associated with penetrating and with the wind, which can penetrate any opening. WHIRLWIND PALMS is characterized by a strong top and a soft bottom, and the body turns like a wheel. Done correctly, this form will help your *ch'i* penetrate every part of your body and make your movements as fast as the wind.

HISTORY AND MASTERS

The origin of Pa-kua is unknown. The first specific reference to it is 1796, when it was recorded that a boxer in Shantung named Wang Hsiang taught the art to a certain Feng Ke-shan. In 1810 Feng met a

Niu Liang-ch'en, who also taught him certain aspects of the art. The traditional teaching, however, is that Tung Hai-ch'uan (1798–1879) of Hopei Province is its modern progenitor.

Tung Hai-ch'uan was a poor boy from Hopei province who, after some scrapes in Peking, journeyed to Mount Omei in Szechwan Province, where he met two Taoists, Ku Chi-tzu and Shang Tao-yuan (the surnames are standard but the given names have strong Taoist connotations, and hence are probably "religious" names), who taught him Pa-kua for eleven years. For seven years he reportedly walked around a tree until it seemed to lean toward him, at which time he became enlightened and reported his experience to the Taoists. They then had him do a figure-8 walk circling two trees, which he did for two years until it seemed that the trees began to "pursue" him. The Taoists praised him and asked if he were homesick. When he acknowledged that he was, they congratulated him on not losing his natural feelings and then taught him hand changes and weapons techniques for two years, after which he returned home to Hopei and then went to Peking, where he taught a number of students.

After becoming famous in Peking, Tung was challenged by Kuo Yun-shen ("Divine Crushing Hand") of the Hsing-i tradition. Throughout two whole days of fighting, Kuo, feared for having killed a man with his famous "crushing" hand, could not gain any advantage. On the third day, Tung took the offensive and so completely defeated Kuo that the two became lifelong friends. They were so impressed with each other's level of accomplishment that they signed a brotherhood pact requiring all their students to train in the other's discipline as well. For this reason—a most unusual outcome for any fight—both Pa-kua and Hsing-i are to this day coupled and complementary.

About the time of the T'ai Ping Rebellion (1850–64), Tung is thought to have been involved in a revolt against the foreign Manchu government, after which he escaped by fleeing to Peking and became an official in the Imperial court. He did not get along with the other officials, however, and was soon thereafter transferred to the household of Prince Su, a relative of Ching-dynasty emperor T'ung Chih (r. 1862–75), to work as a servant, since no one knew of his prowess as a Pa-kua master. Prince Su employed Sha Hui-tsu, a Moslem boxer, as the Chief of the Royal Guards who protected his residence. Sha held every member of the household staff to strict and immediate obedience, and his wife, an expert with a pistol, effectively reinforced her husband's orders. Once, at a crowded banquet, Tung served tea to the guests by lightly scaling the wall and crossing the roof to the kitchen and back. Prince Su recognized from this that Tung must have great ability in some martial art, and subsequently ordered Tung to show his art. Unable to refuse, he demonstrated Pa-kua. His sudden turns and flowing style enthralled the audience. Seeing that, Sha challenged Tung to a fight but was soundly defeated. Thereafter, Tung watched for Sha to try to get revenge. Late one night Sha crept into Tung's bedroom, knife in hand, while his wife aimed her pistol at Tung through the window. Before they were even aware that he was moving, Tung had taken the pistol away from the wife and stood there pointing it at Sha, who thereupon fell to his knees and pounded his head on the floor seeking forgiveness. Tung not only forgave him; he accepted him as a student.

As he aged, he felt the need to pass Pa-kua on and so he retired and began to teach Pa-kua to a few select students. Although Tung gradually withered, the stories about him did not. One tells of how he once found himself surrounded by a group of thugs trying to kill him— but he not only emerged unscathed; he actually defeated the whole band of attackers. Another relates that once Tung was sitting in a chair leaning against a wall when the wall collapsed. His disciples, fearing that he has been buried alive, rushed in looking for him, and found him sitting in the same chair, leaning against another wall! A similar anecdote tells of how he was napping one autumn day and, as the air was quite chilly, his disciples picked up a sheet and quietly tried to cover him. When they put the sheet down, however, there was no one there! "What's the matter with you?" asked Tung's voice from where he was sitting near the window. "Why did you try to startle me?"

But perhaps the grandest story, which is told by Wan Lai-sheng, concerns Tung's death. Certain that he was dead, some of his students attempted to raise the casket prior to the funeral. But it would not budge; it remained as though solidly riveted to the ground. As his students tried again and again to lift it—in vain—a voice came from within, saying: "As I've often said, none of you has even one-tenth my skill!" He then passed away, and the casket was moved easily. Tung died at 81.

Pa-kua emerged from the hidden Taoist ranks first with Tung and only reached the general public after 1900. Among a reported total of only 72, Tung's most famous students were Yin Fu, Ch'eng T'ing-hua, Ma Wei-chi, Liu Feng-ch'un, and Shih Liu.

Yin Fu (nicknamed "Thin Yin") was a native of I-hsien in Hopei Province. Though he had superior skill, he taught few students. He guarded a nobleman's residence for a living and died in 1909 at 69.

Ch'eng T'ing-hua, also a native of Hopei, was nicknamed "Invincible Cobra Ch'eng." Besides teaching Pa-kua, he ran a shop in Peking that sold spectacles, whence he derived his nickname "Cobra." (Europeans, as well, refer to the cobra as the "eyeglass snake"; in German, it is called *brillenschlange*.) One story relates that during the Western occupation of Peking at the time of the Boxer Rebellion (1900), when the foreigners were looting, raping, and killing, Ch'eng rushed out of his house with a knife concealed under each armpit and killed at least a dozen German soldiers before being shot to death. (This story is probably apocryphal, however, since other, more reliable sources assert that he died a natural death past the age of 70.) Another tale tells of how he killed one of his senior students, a man named Ma, who had attacked him while he was in bed.

Ch'eng's top students included Li Ts'un-i, Sun Lu-t'ang, Chang Yu-kuei, Han Ch'i-ying, Feng Chun-i, K'an Ling-feng, Chou Hsiang, Li Han-chang, Li Wen-piao, and Ch'in Ch'eng. Li Ts'un-i, also gifted in Hsing-i, is sometimes recorded as being a direct student of Tung Hai-ch'uan, but his name does not appear on the list engraved on Tung's gravestone. Li, nonetheless, was quite famous and taught thousands in Peking.

Sun Lu-t'ang (1859–1933) learned all three of the internal martial arts, studying Pa-kua under Ch'eng T'ing-hua. Though his interests were diverse, and though he is remembered chiefly for his books—which opened up these arts to the public—he was also a great fighter. Once in Pao-ting, a wrestling stronghold, two opponents simultaneously attacked him, one kicking and one striking. Sun deflected both attacks, and the men were thrown yards away, although bystanders never saw Sun exert any force. At 70, at a boxing meeting, he challenged all present to try to hold on to his finger. Whenever a strong boxer grabbed him with a tight grip, he circularized his *ch'i,* easily extracting the digit from anyone's grasp. Sun's daughter, still alive and teaching T'ai-chi in Peking, recently said that although her father was famous for his fighting, she still remembers how nervous he was a week before a match with a Japanese challenger. He was restless and on edge, awaiting the day. It came, he quickly disposed of the Japanese, and then became his usual calm self again.

Ma Wei-chi, another of Tung's best students, taught Sung Yung-hsiang, Sung Ch'ang-jung, Liu Feng-ch'un, Liang Chen-pu, Chang Chao-tung, and Wang Li-te. Some sources believe that Ma was actually taught by Ch'eng T'ing-hua rather than by Tung himself.

Chang Chao-tung, another native of Hopeh Province, was an expert in both Hsing-i and Pa-kua. Each year Chang returned to his home in Hochien Hsien from Tientsin to visit his parents. The year he turned 60, he returned to find a 40-year-old man named Ma installed as the village's leading boxer. Ma approached Chang and politely told him that he could withstand his punch. (This was the usual way of deciding who was the stronger boxer—each would get a free swing at the other's body. The loser, however, had the choice of challenging for an actual contest if unsatisfied with the one-punch method.) Chang obliged smilingly but ordered four students to hold up a blanket behind Ma. Then he told Ma: "Hold up your hands to protect your body; I will hit only your arm." So saying, Chang hit Ma's arm with his fingers and the back of his hand. Ma immediately fell back sharply into the blanket, pulling all four students atop him. Ma knelt down at once and became a disciple of Chang's.

Wang Shu-chin, the master whose circling method is presented here, started receiving instruction at 18 under the famed Chang Chao-tung in 1923 (Fig. 2). In 1934 he spent a year studying stake standing (*chang chuang*) under Wang Hsiang-chai. Both were "highly skilled, morally upright, and strict taskmasters," he writes in his *Pa-kua Lien-huan Chang* (Pa-kua Linked Palm; Taipei, 1978; privately published. The historical data on Tung Hai-ch'uan are gleaned from this book, and differ somewhat from other accounts. Wang studied in a direct line of succession from Tung, through Ma Wei-chi and Chang Chao-tung; hence, the information he gives is probably more accurate).

Five years later, in 1939, he studied under the 90-year-old veteran Hsiao Hai-po, a master who had studied near Mount Omei in Szechwan, a man who "as a person was genial and cultivated, as a teacher untiring, truly a model for our generation."

Through these years, Wang "avoided entanglements, followed vegetarianism and Taoism, meditated, and practiced boxing." He

2. Wang Shu-chin, Walking the Pa-kua Circle

taught all three internal arts but restricted his Hsing-i and Pa-kua instruction to dedicated students in Taiwan. In the 1960s and 1970s, he went to Japan eight times to teach Tai-chi, and by the time he died in 1981 he had taught nearly 2,000 students, some 1,200 of them in Japan, where he had even opened a branch of his school that still teaches his forms. He was not only a teacher, but a friend. It was his wish that the right method be transmitted in the right way. Therefore, we have taken care to present his method of Pa-kua in a way that we think would have pleased him.

2
Essential Pa-kua

The gulf between what you have already learned and classical Pa-kua is great. The fundmental eight forms of Pa-kua given in this book, with their emphasis on the circular, employ a chiefly *horizontal* strength, in contrast to the mainly linear Hsing-i forms, which develop a more *vertical* strength. If someone attacks you on a straight line with body and legs advancing, that is *vertical* strength. But if you intercept the arm laterally and counterattack on a curving line with your body rotating, that is *horizontal* strength. To help explain the intricacies of classical Pa-kua, we would like to pass on some of the advice given to Mr. Smith by Kuo Feng-ch'ih, under whom he trained for more than two years. The concepts expressed below are intrinsic to all three internal arts and are in accord with the principles of the art as taught by Wang. Thus, if you understand these ideas, you will comprehend the rationale of T'ai-chi and Hsing-i, as well as Pa-kua.

SUBSTANCE AND FUNCTION

To eradicate any erroneous ideas you may have, let us compare both the *internal* and the *external* types of martial arts. If we examine the substance and function of the two types of boxing, we will see that there is a great difference between them.

All *internal* styles are based on the combined training of body and spirit, as exemplified in Taoist doctrines, the main goal of which is to achieve a state of being without any desire or belligerent attitude, neither self-abasing nor arrogant, always advancing and indomitable. In the *internal* styles, "spiritual" cultivation and the nurturing of *ch'i* are primary, but boxing theory, technique, and practice must also be accorded their due. When the need arises, the "spiritual" cultivation is transmuted into physical activity in exactly the right amount needed to protect you from harm.

All the *external* styles, however, place more stress on the physical training aspect, emphasizing muscle size and strength, as well as the achievement of impractical feats of physical prowess. They tend to flamboyant displays and demonstrations of sheer strength.

Visually, the two types of boxing appear the same to the average layman, except that sometimes the *internal* styles look too slow to be effective as self-defense systems. In reality, quite the opposite is true. In fact, muscular training as espoused by the *external* styles is restricted by age, whereas the spiritual development of the *internal* styles continues through life, actually becoming deeper and more profound with age. It is undeniable that often the use of a single part of the body in *external* boxing is admirable—but it requires much time and effort to perform it correctly, and the use of it often leaves other parts of the body open to attack. The strength of *internal* boxing, however, is hidden, and permeates everything in equal proportions. Stored within the body, the *ch'i* is virtually inexhaustible and can be gathered for use. Not being localized in any particular part of the body, the strength can suddenly shoot forth from any quarter.

In the practical application of the two styles, too, there are many other differences in terms of principles and methods. The *internal* styles are based upon *change*, upon the interplay of *yin* and *yang*, and upon how to win without resorting to violence. A master of an *internal* form can dodge, deflect, and counterattack instinctively, because his mental training has made him ready for anything.

An ancient boxing classic states: "Boxing is like taking a walk; striking an enemy is like snapping your fingers." This is not to belittle the power of the *external* forms. When an *external* master is in his prime, he is a veritable fighting machine. But machines break down with wear and tear and with age. The *internal* styles, in contrast, not only protect one through automatic self-defense mechanisms; they also bring health, and can be said, therefore, to teach both fighting and living skills at the same time.

CONCEPTS NEEDED FOR PRACTICE

A novice needs a strong desire to learn, confidence that he can eventually master the form, and the understanding to appreciate its function. He must be prepared both mentally and physically, and he must have the proper concept in mind. He is like a man setting off upon a journey—if he wants to reach his destination quickly and safely, he will choose the best transport and the shortest route. In the *internal* styles, however, the student is ultimately on a journey to discover himself.

The ideal student is one of middle age, since he has accumulated much knowledge and experience while growing. Confucius said: "A person at forty will not be diverted." This originally referred to ethical cultivation, but can be applied to any kind of learning. When young, a person tends to show off strength, but when he is older his strength will eventually fail him. Then he knows that what he had earlier was superficial and of no use to him. Guilt and regret then impel him to learn the art from the beginning. Now more quiet than when young, he turns to the spiritual aspect of the art and gains tranquility. To learn an *internal* art correctly, a student must do only one thing—*nothing* that is unnatural. (In Chinese, it is said that he must have *wu-wei*—the virtue of "doing nothing" that is not natural or spontaneous.) This ability to "do nothing" brings harmony to life, but takes a long time and great effort to achieve.

Wrong ideas can mislead the student—and they are rampant. Many divide the *internal* schools into *hard, soft,* and *change,* equating Hsing-i with *hard,* T'ai-chi with *soft,* and Pa-kua with *change.* On one level of discussion, this may be right; but when seen with a broader perspective this is far from correct. Others say that Hsing-i is for youngsters; Pa-kua, for the middle-aged; and T'ai-chi, for the old. How absurd! The three are actually joined together in a more intricate trinity—they are but three aspects of the same truth. From Hsing-i, you can learn the physical aspects of the *internal* function, while you can reach the spiritual essence of *internal boxing* from T'ai-chi and Pa-kua, providing that you study for years under a competent teacher, during which you work yourself to the limit of your ability.

All three of the *internal* martial arts are based on *i,* the will or the mind. The mind is the source of all action. The idea is to keep the mind still while the body moves. To remain still while the body moves in a linear fashion—that is Hsing-i; and to do so while the body moves in circles—that is Pa-kua. The idea is formed and the body moves in accord with the mind. *Hard* and *soft* are merely points of transition, extremes that are constantly in the process of turning into their opposites. Thus, it is wrong to say that one of these arts is *hard,* and another *soft.*

To learn the *internal* arts properly, then, the mind must dominate the body. At first, the student must adopt *wu-wei* and forget the self. Then he must go on to not only accept but even to embody these radical principles:

1. Boxing requires movement, but, first, the *internal* requires stillness;

2. To defeat an opponent requires strength, but, first, the *internal* requires softness;
3. Fighting requires speed, but, first, the *internal* requires slowness.

These basic three axioms comprise the best mode of transport for bringing the student quickly and easily to his goal. If he follows the principle of "To know first, to act second," rather than blindly going through the actions without any awareness of what he is doing, his achievement will be great.

NOTES ON PRACTICE

Beginners should be familiar with the standards of training as set down by the old masters. Training was and is the heart of the art. Knowledge cannot replace training, though it can improve the manner in which you train. When boxing and the other combative arts of China were at their zenith, men trained as though their lives depended on it. Many of them were convoy guards, and their lives did depend on the skills they honed over the years. Old masters insisted upon twenty years to learn the art of Pa-kua. The regimen of training often required six hours a day and included exhaustive solo forms, bag work, two-man exercises, and work with an arsenal of weapons. The study of martial skills required an athletic capacity now superseded by the invention of the gun.

Although the internal arts avoided feats of physical prowess, training in them was no less exhausting. It tested the nerve and the will of the student and left deep physical and psychological marks. But the skills forged over the years were absorbed into the person's nervous system, leaving no outward sign of extraordinary ability.

Nowadays, even with lower standards, training in internal boxing still requires at least one hour daily, six days a week. In this way, a degree of physical strength is maintained and mingled with a spirit of enquiry. With time, the two are fired by your growing commitment and produce a forged skill. In the first ten years of training, the beginner should do about twenty to thirty repetitions of the eight palm changes, in addition to the auxiliary exercises, on each day set aside for practice.

Practice should be done outside in natural surroundings, which encourage your body to acclimatize itself to natural conditions and help the mind to become calm. The best time for practice is around sunrise, when the air is fresh, the light penetrating, and the mind quiet. For relaxation and concentration, the area should be as private as possible. Observers distract and detract. Silence in a noisy world is rare, but it is also essential for sharpening and quieting your nerves; thus, pay attention to the postures and not to music or other things.

Begin practice gradually, and, as your body warms up, bend your legs more, take longer steps, and extend your arms. Once warmed up, speed should approximate brisk walking. If the movement is done too slowly, rhythm will not reveal itself; if too fast, the postures will lose clarity and crispness, creating confusion in the mind rather than relaxation. The rhythm should help to regulate the emotions. Speed is a result and not a goal—it comes only as a result of finely honed coordination and kinesiological economy.

Above all, the only way to prevent your postures from becoming mere mechanical performance is to keep your mind on your *tan-t'ien* and to relax unnecessary tension, thereby opening up your body, increasing your breathing capacity, and quickening the flow of *ch'i*. Through long practice, this leads to finely tuned synchronization of your muscular contractions (bodily movements) and in the end improves your mind.

An alternate form of learning the postures endorsed by the old masters is that of pausing several times in each posture while steadying the breath and the body. This allows the mind to focus on the body parts, to find and eliminate unnecessary tensions, and to sensitize the mind to the postural mistakes it must correct. The effects of gravity become more familiar as the mind comes to see more clearly how it relates to the body, and thus mechanical efficiency increases. The stress of static postures on the legs strengthens them and increases their flexibility and stamina. This also strengthens the tendons of the whole body from the toes to the fingertips. Some teachers advise counting the breaths for various periods of time, other simply pause for a moment. Breathe naturally, embracing the *ch'i* in the *tan-t'ien* while holding a posture.

Initially, the mind will rebel against holding the postures, and the muscles will ache, but, with repetition, the mind will adjust. For the mind to be still, first the body must be still. It is then that the sense of stillness comes. This teaches the student something of the discipline of the will and the value of silent stillness.

At the turn of the century, when leading boxers often worked as guards and were all-around combat experts, they used calisthenics and other forms of conditioning. The Taoists, however, emphasized the principle of naturalness in their internal arts that sought simplicity, eschewing artifice of any kind. At times, ancillary training is useful as a therapeutic tool, as swimming is for arthritis and calisthenics and weight training are for scoliosis. Though it may be a necessity, this type of therapeutic training will not develop the skill born of naturalness that the postures and training are designed to develop. "Auxiliary training," or training that is directed toward competitive ends and performance in public is unnecessary. Weight training, if organized around the postures and their principles, can be useful but is also unnecessary.

THE TEACHER-STUDENT RELATIONSHIP

Success in internal boxing often depends upon the relationship between the teacher and the student. Traditionally, this relationship was
much like that of father and son. This aspect of the Chinese martial
arts has not traveled well into commercial America, but a few words
about this important relationship may help readers to understand an
art decidedly different from the Hollywood nonsense seen in film,
television, and the printed media.

The relationship between a student and his teacher derives from
cultural mores based largely upon Confucian teachings on filial piety
and family. Thus, in studying the internal arts, all the students of the
same teacher regard themselves as brothers, with seniority based upon
age and experience. They revere and respect the teacher and help him
as needed in his daily life.

The intention of the teacher and the student must agree in order for
the teaching to "take." This requires time and mutual trust. This
trust must evolve out of respect and is reflected in mature self-restraint
and behavior—and an occasional errand or gift. If a student's
behavior is lacking, the teacher will abridge or withhold the teaching.
Thus, transmission of the art requires not only respect but
perseverance while respect is being worked out. The student at first
acts out of courtesy but gradually comes to an attitude of genuinely car-
ing for the teacher and following his guidance and doing whatever he
can to help him. This earns the teaching. The technique, however,
must be worked out through long, consistent training in which the
teacher observes and disciplines the student's behavior, thus prevent-
ing the "right means from working in the wrong way"—that is,
through teaching the art to the wrong person.

For his part, the superior teacher paces the teaching, giving the student what can be learned in a given period, praising effort and cen-

suring idleness. He should welcome new students as adventures and not be afraid to stop teaching those too egocentric to learn. By and large, the relationship should make both parties more productive and happier—and, as Bertrand Russell once wrote, the Chinese prefer happiness to power (would that we could all be satisfied with that).

PART TWO   Pa-kua Training

3

The Basics

Although Hsing-i is largely linear and fisted and Pa-kua circular and open-palmed, the philosophy and principles of one apply equally to the other. Both occupy moral bases established by Confucius and Lao-tzu. Teaching different doctrines, both men sought to produce a just man following a virtuous way—Confucius, through a macrocosmic social contract built on the family; Lao-tzu, through a societal perfection coming from a microcosmic individual effort to realize oneself. Confucius wanted to regulate society, while Lao-tzu sought to advise the individual. Confucius taught behavior, Lao-tzu taught correct breathing and hygiene.

And, like the other internal arts, Pa-kua teaches boxing as a discipline, not as an excuse to contend with others. The great master Teng Yun-feng once explained to a class in Peking that Pa-kua should be used to neutralize attacks but that the secret was *never to use it*. When a feisty student questioned, "Why, then, learn it?" Teng countered with, "If you don't want to learn it, get out of here." What he was saying is that while Pa-kua is permeated with self-defensive functions, one must avoid even the occasion of having to cause distress to another.

THE MAIN PRINCIPLES

Pa-kua is not an easy art to master. Although it can be learned in less time than the twenty years the old masters insisted upon, it does require regular and tedious practice over a period of several years. Chou Chi-ch'un, one of the leading modern historians of the Chinese martial arts, once said:

> Pa-kua is difficult to learn. You walk very slowly for two or three years, then go faster and, later, very fast. The chief aims are to move behind an opponent quickly and to strengthen the arms. Through the practice, heavy weights can later be attached to the arms without discomfort. At the turn of the century, a famous master went to Japan and, while there, supported the weight of a sumo wrestler on his outstretched arm! Often, accomplished boxers would carry a cup of tea in each palm while spinning and turning their bodies—all without spilling a single drop!

The most important principles of Pa-kua are:

1. *Move your body naturally.* The best rule to help you do this is to follow all the other rules. Avoid the rudimentary Shaolin and karate exercises, as they will only make you stiff and exhausted. The muscle building they encourage impedes the proper flow of *ch'i* in the body as well as its coordination and celerity of movement.

2. *Stretch your arm but withdraw your trapezius muscle.* (Although this may seem contradictory or antagonistic, it is an important part of Pakua. *See* "Internally Bound, Externally Stretched," below.) This strengthens the flow of *ch'i*. Another similar posture is to lower your waist by "holding" downward the small of the back muscles while also "feeling" the sacrum as if it were ready to spring up.

3. *Harmonize your vital energy and your strength.* Internal boxing insists that three things must be coordinated: the mind (*i*) must command, the strength (*li*) must obey, and the vital energy (*ch'i*) must follow. In the internal forms, *internal* truths must be transformed into

The Twelve Basic Principles

1. Clear your mind and keep your head erect and your neck straight. Look directly ahead.

2. Round your shoulders slightly, hollowing your chest and easing the movement of *ch'i*.

3. Turn your upper thighs slightly inward, protecting the lower navel so that the air can go deeply.

4. Breathe long and slowly through your nose.

5. To let your nerves function naturally, keep your body erect from the neck to the tip of your coccyx.

6. Relax your waist, tuck the tip of your coccyx in and upward, and slightly contract the sphincter muscle.

7. Sink your shoulders and drop your elbows. Only if your elbows hang can your shoulders sink, and only if your shoulders sink can *ch'i* go to your fingertips.

8. Touch your tongue to the roof of your mouth, close your mouth lightly, and let your teeth meet without pressure lest the *ch'i* be retarded. Then, exercise will produce saliva, which will irrigate the throat.

9. Pa-kua comes from the mind. It blends the external strength (*li*) and the internal energy (*ching*), thus enabling us to "seek stillness in movement."

10. Pa-kua walking is done, not with the legs straight, but with "sitting thighs," with the legs well bent. In walking, keep your feet low and "button" (*k'ou*—with your toes slightly inward) downward, causing your soles to cup the ground flatly as if walking in mud. When you walk, your front foot touches lightly, and when the rear foot is flat, it feels as if you are pushing down as in climbing a mountain. The ankle of your advancing foot brushes the other ankle as it passes. After a while your step will be as light and fast as running water.

11. Your waist is the big axis and is used to mobilize, stimulate, and move the four extremities. Before your body moves, your waist moves (Fig. 6).

12. In the basic palm, "Lotus-leaf Palm," keep your fingers separated and your palm concave. Your thumb is held horizontally, your index finger vertically, and your remaining fingers are proportionally bent so that your thumb, index finger, and little finger form a triangle.

The Ten Prohibitions

AVOID:

1. Pride and vanity.
2. Excessive physical desires and irregular hours.
3. Strong alcoholic beverages, drugs, and stimulants.
4. Practicing when too tense or tired.
5. Practicing in dead or polluted air.
6. Practicing in a strong wind; for rooting exercises, practice in a windless place.
7. Practicing right after eating.
8. Exerting so much *ch'i* in practicing that your strength is blunted.
9. Practicing movements and odd postures out of their natural sequence.
10. Immediately after practice: leaving on wet clothes in a draft; sitting or lying down; eating, drinking, or smoking, or going to the toilet.

external boxing forms, suggesting that thought and action must work in unison.

4. *Keep your* ch'i *concentrated in the* tan-t'ien *below the navel.* This psychic energy center (about three inches below the navel) should also mark your true center of gravity. To concentrate the vital energy there means to "sink" your strength from the upper to the lower torso in order to gain stability.

"INTERNALLY BOUND, EXTERNALLY STRETCHED"

Wang Shu-chin stressed the principle of *nei-kuo, wai-ch'eng* (internally bound, externally stretched), a maxim describing a kinesiological sense developed from long practice walking the circle (Fig. 3). "Internal binding" refers to the feeling produced by the muscles and connective tissue linking the upper torso to the area of the *tan-t'ien*, just below the

3. Wang Shu-chin Doing the "Squatting Tiger" of Pa-kua

navel, which corresponds also to the body's center of gravity. Surrounding this area and supporting its organs are the muscular sheathing of the abdomen, the omentum of the intestines, the *quadratus lumborum*, and the anchoring tendons of the diaphragm, which stretch upward from the lumbar spine to the costal margin forming a dome over the viscera. This network of muscles and supporting tissue produces a tugging sensation around the *tan-t'ien* as though it were a bag being pulled slightly by connecting fibers. The tugging or bound/wrapped sensation is not produced by over-articulation so much as by simply doing and feeling the postures.

"External stretching" is evident in the antagonistic articulation of the hand, wrist, and elbow. When extended, the arms stretch the tendons by keeping the shoulders and elbows down. The scapulae do not slide forward and the chest is not contracted but held naturally. The breath is directed mentally down to the navel, and up through the diaphragm and lungs. Correct breathing feels as if the whole torso is inflating like a bellows. Inflating the lungs expands the ribs coincident with the downward pull of the diaphragm, which presses on the intestines and the *tan-t'ien* area, producing the feeling in the torso of "internally bound, externally stretched." (Fig. 4).

The deep breathing, antagonistically extended arms, upright torso, and low center of gravity (achieved by bending the legs) combine with the kinesthetics of moving on a double circle (circling with yourself as pivot, and turning around an external circle), swinging, rolling, and spinning, to provide the holistic and very real feel of this dynamic and pervasive principle. Stated simply, the internal binding (or sinking) counterbalances the energy you direct through your arms outward toward the center of the circle. Functionally, this adds to your root and prevents an opponent from countering your external energy. Meditationally, it sinks, nourishes, and maintains your *ch'i*, your mind, and your *tan-t'ien* (Figs. 5, 6).

4. Author Smith Punching Wang Shu-chin (1960)

5. Wang Shu-chin Doing the ''Hawk'' of Pa-kua

6. Wang Shu-chin Doing the ''Monkey'' of Pa-kua

THE NINE PALACES

The idea of "Nine Palaces" is both practical and esoteric. It derives from ancient Taoist cosmology and dance. Originally, it signified nine stations or portals that adepts would dance among, sealing off this dimension from evil outside influences. Nine is an auspicious number to Asians, and among the Cabalists is regarded as the number of powers under God. In Chinese boxing, the number nine is used in the names of boxing styles as diverse as Little Nine-Heaven Boxing (*Hsiao Chiu T'ien Ch'uan*) and Cheng Man-ch'ing's version of Yang-style T'ai-chi, in which emphasis is put on opening the nine joints or parts of the body (the top of the head, the neck, the wrists, the elbows, the shoulders, the hips, the sacrum, the knees, and the ankles), and in which the development of one's skill passes through nine phases.

The cosmic dance found its way into Pa-kua boxing as a practical means to develop footwork fluency while extending the exercise from a single circle to a figure-8 (Fig. 7) to a nine-station regimen (Fig. 8).

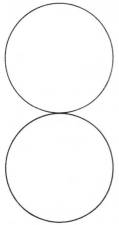

7. The Pa-kua Figure-8

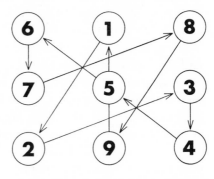

8. The Pa-kua Nine Stations

The nine palaces also portray the $3 \times 3 = 9$ relativity of the body divided into three corresponding sets of bases, centers, and tips:

1. The upper body has the shoulders as the base, the elbows as the center, and the hands as the tip.

2. The lower body has the hips as the base, the knees as the center, and the feet as the tip.

3. The whole body has the *tan-t'ien* (seat of power) as the base, the heart (seat of emotion) as the center, and the head (seat of intelligence) as the tip.

	Base	*Center*	*Tip*
Upper body	Shoulders	Elbows	Hands
Lower body	Hips	Knees	Feet
Whole body	*Tan-t'ien*	Heart	Head

In Pa-kua, the sets are further tactically divided into the high, middle, and low techniques. The head is the high or "heavenly" tip penetrating the skies. The spirit rises and the essences can combine harmoniously in one place. The torso is the middle set: if it stays erect and does not lean, the nervous system can respond quickly and the *ch'i* can flow easily. The feet are the low or "earthly" base, so important for stability and agility. The student must distinguish three sections: the head is the tip; the torso, the center; and the feet, the base—the head must be sure; the body, well rooted; and the feet, fluent. If any are awry, the mind (*i*) cannot function properly. All is one. Pa-kua's power comes from all components of the body coordinating with the mind and with the *ch'i*. This coming together is the meaning of the old phrase, "The Nine Palaces return to one."

Sun Lu-t'ang, in his *Pa-kua ch'uan hsueh* [A Study of Pa-kua Boxing; Peking, 1916], touches on the esoteric aspect of the Nine Palaces as follows (paraphrased):

> The Nine Palaces are a cosmological arrangement and are not unique to Pa-kua boxing. They are found in *Chi Men Ch'uan* (Mysterious Gate Boxing), which also has movements around nine stations.... The Nine Palaces are the points of integration whereby the prebirth (*hsien-t'ien*) and the postbirth (*hou-t'ien*) energies [those you are born with and those you develop] unite. The purpose of the Nine Palaces is to enable the student to obey the divine will (*i*). When the Nine Palaces are integrated, you are ready for the final stage, the "great awakening."
>
> The Nine Palaces are realized best when the upper/lower and inner/outer aspects of a student are harmonized. As the years pass, his whole being is reformed. His sinews and membranes change continuously, coming under more direct control of his brain. In turn, his brain then is controlled by his spirit, and, ultimately, by the divine mind, or the *tao*.
>
> As this process occurs, the student occasionally will glimpse his original or divine face for a moment. This moment must recur many times for him to be able to progress to the final phase, in which he can will the divine face to reappear. Therefore, one who trains at Pa-kua diligently for a considerable amount of time displays his nature at its best.

Do not be concerned if the subject of what Sun spoke of seems too esoteric or abstruse. It is not important that you understand every idea—especially at the beginning. Merely do the practice as set forth in Part Two, and, over time, your body will help your mind to come to an understanding.

OTHER PRINCIPLES

Kuo Feng-ch'ih once said that it is easy for a weak person or one who knows nothing of boxing at all to learn Pa-kua. Such a person is not preoccupied with past instruction and does not resist the advice given but merely goes ahead and follows it. Boxing masters advise that three requirements must be followed in learning Pa-kua:

1.   You should remain *relaxed*. If you are tense, your mind can neither think calmly nor react quickly. If your body is tense, your motions will be sluggish and you will be slow to respond. With relaxation your mind will be liberated and your body will attain a happy, unencumbered circulation of air and blood.

2.   You should heed the *slow*, a word that refers not only to action but also to a state of mind free from impatience and anxiety. Slowness harmonizes outside and inside influences. By beginning slowly, you as a novice will have sufficient time *to seek, listen to, feel for,* and *apprehend* the essence of Pa-kua and for your body to adjust itself, various muscles reforming themselves in line with your practice. Gradually, the action will become faster, but your internal focus will remain as slow and as steady as when you did it slowly.

3.   You should strive for *evenness* of actions and breathing. Pa-kua will prevent erratic and unbalanced movements by teaching you to sink your breath to your *tan-t'ien*, which will permit normal breathing even when you are moving strenuously. Practice itself will harmonize action and breathing. You adjust your breathing unconsciously in time to slow or fast movement, just as we unconsciously adjust our breathing while eating. Pa-kua, like eating, is natural, and regulates the breath in the same way. It stresses naturalness; teachers often tell their students to observe children and to breathe naturally as they do.

4.   Keep your chest relaxed, not held out in a military fashion, to help the circulation of your *ch'i*. Hold your tongue so that the tip

touches the hard palate (the roof of the mouth) and hold your head straight (as though a string from the ceiling were attached to the center of your head). Expand or round your back by dropping your shoulders; drop your elbows, too, when extending your arms.

5. Master the techniques of:

Rise (*ch'i*)—start to raise your right hand;

Drill (*tsuan*)—as it ascends, turn the palm upward in a clockwise drilling strike;

Fall (*lo*)—begin to lower your hand, palm still up;

Overturn (*fan*)—as it descends, twist the right palm downward in a counterclockwise strike or grasp.

4
Walking the Circle

THE CONCEPT OF THE CIRCLE

The essence of Pa-kua is to be found in the circling movement and in its changes. The practice is based upon "walking the circle," which means that you should walk around an imaginary or a marked circle and periodically change direction.

Everything in nature tends to be circular: the sun, the moon, the cycles of the seasons. And a baby's smile. Even straight lines are only shorter segments of a bigger circle. The underlying Taoist principles with the palm changes correlated to the eight *kua* in an endless circle provide an exercise of the whole person in managing his body in peace or struggle. As you walk the circle, the exercise becomes a link to psycho-physiological processes that increase your knowledge of yourself. This knowledge then results in apperception of the relationship between the macrocosm and the microcosm; thus Pa-kua ends by blending meditation and self-defense, an exercise in handling reality.

Pa-kua reflects the universe: the universe turns; the weather rolls; we walk. When you walk around the circle, you walk the universe and your inscape at the same time. Your thoughts derive from the universe, and they expand until thought and action become one. Perceive and know your mind, for it directs thought like a canal directs water. And when you know your mind and its adaptations to circumstances, you can direct it. The person who can handle the rigor

9. Author Smith, Walking the Pa-kua Circle

and continuous change of Pa-kua can live with the ambiguities of life: he has gained the intelligence of the art.

Walking the circle is the chief exercise in Pa-kua. You walk the circle for a few minutes or hours, your body erect, legs well bent, *ch'i* at the *tan-t'ien,* and your arms exerting "internally bound, externally stretched'' energy (Fig. 9). Periodically, you change hands and body, holding the same posture while you circle in the opposite direction.

Begin with a circle six to twelve feet in diameter, and as you progress, reduce it, commensurate with your skill. Initially walk with your knees slightly bent, and as your body warms up bend them more. The lowest height and most difficult position puts you in a sitting posture—it is said that the old-timers practiced in a room with only a five-foot ceiling—but the middle height we use here is the most useful. It develops leg strength without sacrificing mobility and develops the knee muscles and ligaments—a prerequisite for the lowest walking.

To maximize the effect of circle walking, experiment with several steps. You may begin by suspending your rear foot and pausing at the front ankle to develop stability. Or you may walk by touching the rear foot down forward in a ''false'' step and then making the step slightly longer before transferring your weight onto the foot. Finally, using the separation principle of Tai-chi, you may step forward, putting your entire sole on the floor before weighting it. This is difficult and must be done slowly and in a low posture for best results. Practicing long and short steps is also encouraged, so that you may better analyze uses. Also, lifting the knees high in walking develops kicking skills while resting the lower back. At first, speed can be an impediment. It is better to integrate the basics at a slow or moderate pace before adding speed.

The circle itself can be changed in various ways beyond the simple clockwise and counterclockwise. After walking circles of varying sizes, accustoming your legs to the regimen, and practicing the changes, increase the complexity by walking a figure-8 (Fig. 7), linking the two circles at the intersection. When this is mastered, walk through each of nine stations, circling each (Fig. 8). Go in both directions and arbitrarily use whatever posture you wish, but always feel the presence of an opponent. This will add variety to your Pa-kua.

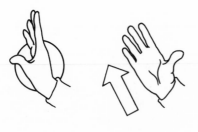

1. STANDING   2. CARRYING   3. SUPPORTING   4. CUTTING

THE EIGHT MAJOR PALM SHAPES

Force in Pa-kua is transmitted to the target in circular movements through the legs, body, and hands using the body weight and rooting. The body is an avenue that must be kept clear, through which the mind directs the *ch'i*. The final impact is enhanced by articulating the palms into eight major shapes (Fig. 10). Often, one shape will lead into or follow another in a response sequence.

1.   STANDING PALM   exemplifies the Pa-kua maxim "internally bound, externally stretched." The hand, wrist, and elbow all have this strength. This palm is used in the basic walking posture around the circle. Excellent for strengthening the tendons of the arms as well as the spine, it may be articulated as a deflection, a push to the body, or a "blinder" slap or as a strike to the head or chin. Wang called this hand style, in which the thumb and little finger form a triangle, the "Lotus-leaf Palm."

2.   CARRYING PALM   can be used as a chop to vital points, or as a push upward or directly ahead. It may also be used as a combined deflection-attack, as in the T'ai-chi postures called FAIR LADY WORKS AT SHUTTLES, and also is part of the Pa-kua form named WHITE SNAKE STICKS OUT TONGUE, in which one hand serves as a block while the other strikes simultaneously beneath it.

3.   SUPPORTING PALM   is a pushing or spearing strike depending on whether or not the fingers are held pointing straight out or downward. It is fused into most of the change patterns as a sequential   movement   (for   example,   in   WHITE   MONKEY

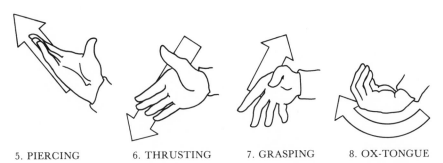

5. PIERCING   6. THRUSTING   7. GRASPING   8. OX-TONGUE

10. The Eight Major Palm Shapes

PRESENTS A PEACH, you may use SUPPORTING PALMS to push the opponent's lower abdomen before lifting the hands up into PIERCING PALMS). It may also be employed as an upholding deflection and will balance the centrifugal force of your body when moving and turning.

4. CUTTING PALM   is a lateral chop with a scraping action. It combines the hand edge with pressing forward and can be articulated into a clamp. A major tactic of Pa-kua, it is seen in the initial chop in the SQUATTING TIGER form of the SINGLE CHANGE OF PALM.

5. PIERCING PALM   penetrates with the fingers in a drilling or screwing action. It is seen in SINGLE CHANGE OF PALM, in which, after chopping, you may turn your palm to pierce with your fingers. It is also used to attack the opponent's external obliques or to jostle him on a vertical axis.

6. THRUSTING PALM   is a vertical chopping downward seen especially in GIANT ROC SPREADS WINGS, but it may also be used as a deflection.

7. GRASPING PALM   corresponds to the WARD OFF of T'ai-chi. It is used to grasp the opponent's wrist, elbow, shoulder, throat, belt, or leg. The retracting hand is invariably GRASPING PALM. Articulated, it can be held palm in or out. It is seen in the swing back out of SINGLE CHANGE OF PALM, after the first PIERCING of DOUBLE CHANGE OF PALM, and in the first high deflection of HAWK SOARS UP TO HEAVEN.

8. OX-TONGUE PALM   corresponds to the T'ai-chi posture called SINGLE WHIP; it is used to poke with the fingers or to strike/ deflect with the back of the wrist.

THE EIGHT CHANGES

1. SINGLE CHANGE OF PALM (*Tan Huan Chang*)
Start by standing erect, feet held with toes 45° apart, heels together and left foot facing straight ahead, on the circumference of the circle (Fig. 11). Raise your arms outward, palms down (Fig. 12), and, as they come up to shoulder level, turn your palms up (Fig. 13). Continuing, raise your hands overhead till they face (Fig. 14). Now shift most of your weight to your right foot, turn your upper torso leftward, your left palm pressing out, your right palm pressing down (Fig. 15). Shifting the rest of your weight to your right foot, put your left foot down on the circle ahead as your left and right palms continue pressing outward and down, respectively (Fig. 16). Stay erect, sinking the shoulders, elbows, and body.

Walk with your left hand focused on the center of the circle. Your feet are so close that your ankles brush in passing, the advancing foot touching down heel first. Begin each change by bringing your outside foot forward and toeing it in (usually) or out (only in YELLOW DRAGON ROLLS OVER). To change here, bring your right foot forward and toe it in ahead of your left without changing your palms (Fig. 17). Shift your weight to your right foot and turn your waist leftward while your left foot pivots on the ball (Fig. 18). Now step forward with your left foot, your left hand CUTTING forward while your right hand GRASPS, palm up, and retracts to your right side (Fig. 19). This posture is 60% rear-weighted and is called SQUATTING TIGER.

Now toe-out and transfer your weight to your left foot as you suspend your right foot near your left ankle and PIERCE your left armpit with your right hand, palm up, "embracing" your left shoulder, your body twisting slightly leftward (Fig. 20). As you turn rightward back toward the center, your right hand goes from under your left arm and slightly upward, while your left hand turns over, palm up, near your

11 12 13

14 15 16

17 18 19

20

21

22

23

right elbow and both arms swing back rightward (Fig. 21). As your right palm continues its turn toward the center, extend your right leg, the toes down, and sit, sinking squarely down on your pelvis (Fig. 22). For those familiar with T'ai-chi, on this swing you protect by presenting two WARD OFFS—with the arm and the leg—to the center. In Wang's system, the knee is brought higher than in others. Put your foot down on the circle and walk, your right palm turning gradually with your torso to the center and your left palm pressing down (Fig. 23).

24

2. DOUBLE CHANGE OF PALM (*Shuang Huan Chang*)
Walking the circle with your left palm focused on the center (Fig. 24),
toe-in your right foot and begin as in SINGLE CHANGE (Figs. 25, 26),
pausing at SQUATTING TIGER (Fig. 27). Toe-out your left foot,
depress with your left palm, and step forward with your right foot,
PIERCING your right hand, palm up, over your depressing left palm
(Figs. 28, 29).

Now toe-in your right foot, turn your waist leftward, and take your
right hand high, your palm down, "folding" (Fig. 30). Simultane-

25

26

27

28

29

30

31

32

ously, move your left hand, palm up, near your left waist, shift your weight to your right foot, and suspend your left foot at your right ankle (Fig. 31). Step backward with your left foot, pivoting on your right heel, and squat, scraping your left hand, palm up, down your left leg toward your ankle (Fig. 32). Drop your right hand, palm down, near your left elbow.

Next, toe-out your left foot slightly and shift your weight onto it. At the same time, turn your left hand over and press the palm edge for-

33

34

ward in CUTTING as you rise, your right hand following your left elbow (Fig. 33). Transfer all your weight to your left foot, PIERCING with your right palm upward under your left armpit and suspending your right foot at your left ankle (Fig. 34). Swinging rightward toward the center, raise your right knee high, extending your right palm forward and pressing your left palm down (Fig. 35), and continue to walk the circle (Fig. 36), gradually turning your torso and hands toward the center.

35

36

37   38   39

40   41

3. HAWK SOARS UP TO HEAVEN (*Yao Fei Li T'ien*)

This change is also called UP-AND-DOWN CHANGE PALMS (*Shang-hsia huan chang*). Walking with your left hand focused on the center (Fig. 37), toe-in your right foot deeply (Fig. 38). Then toe-out your left foot in a short step leftward and raise your left hand high with the palm out in GRASPING (Fig. 39). Step forward and toe-in your right foot, your back toward the center, and SPEAR your right hand, palm in, over your left, palm down, at your right elbow (Fig. 40). This right spear can use either the CARRYING or the GRASPING palm.

Next, pivot on your right heel leftward and suspend your left foot at your right ankle (Fig. 41). Then step backward to the circle with your left foot, squatting on your right leg, and CUT with both of your palms. Your right hand is higher than your left, which is aligned with

42

43

44

45

your left leg, and you are 85% rear-weighted (Fig. 42). Toe-out your left foot as in DOUBLE CHANGE OF PALM, rise, and shift your weight to it, CUTTING forward with your left palm edge while holding your right hand, palm up, at your right hip (Fig. 43).

Finally, do SINGLE CHANGE OF PALM as before, PIERCING with your right palm under your left armpit, turning leftward, and suspending your right foot at your left ankle (Fig. 44). Swing rightward, separating your hands, carrying your right knee high (Fig. 45), and, as your right palm stretches toward the center, put your right foot down (Fig. 46). Then continue to walk the circle, gradually turning your torso and hands toward the center.

46

47

48

4. YELLOW DRAGON ROLLS OVER (*Huang Lung Fan Shen*)

DRAGON is the only change in which you toe-out with your outside foot as it comes forward instead of toeing-in as usual. Walking with your left palm focused on the center (Fig. 47), make an extreme toe-out with your right foot (Fig. 48) and shift your weight onto it until your left foot comes up on its toes. Then step forward with your left foot parallel to your right in a HORSE STANCE. Your back is now to

49   50   51

52   53

the center, your left palm forward at ear level, and your right hand, palm down, near your navel (Fig. 49). Shift your weight to your left foot and suspend your right foot at your left knee, extending your left hand, palm edge CUTTING forward, at eyebrow level, your right hand at your left armpit, as you lean forward (Fig. 50). Finally, twist your body slightly leftward, taking your right hand, palm up, under your left armpit (Fig. 51), then swing rightward, raising your knee, your right palm out as before, in SINGLE CHANGE OF PALM (Figs. 52, 53). Then walk the circle, gradually turning your torso and hands toward the center.

54 55 56

57 58

5. WHITE SNAKE STICKS OUT TONGUE (*Pai She T'u Shen*)
Walking with your left hand toward the center of the circle (Fig. 54),
toe-in your right foot (Fig. 55). Swing your bent left arm down and to
the right with your waist (Fig. 56). As you shift your weight onto your
right foot, take your left hand, palm out, and move it in a large
counterclockwise circle overhead (Fig. 57), turning your waist leftward, and ending with your left hand palm up and at chin level, in
PIERCING palm, and your right hand palm up, in GRASPING palm,
near your right hip (Fig. 58). Most of your weight is on your right foot;
your left is placed so that only the ball of the foot touches the ground.

Take a half-step forward with your left foot, while your left hand,
palm up, PIERCES, your weight 60% rear-loaded (Fig. 59). Toe-out
your left foot, press your left palm down, and step forward with your

59

60   61   62

63   64

right foot while PIERCING with your right hand, palm up, over your depressing left palm (Figs. 60, 61). Your weight is again 60% rear-weighted. Now shift your weight to your left foot, toe-in your right foot, and raise your right hand high, palm down, GRASPING, while bringing your left hand, palm up, near your left hip (Fig. 62).

Now shift your weight to your right foot and suspend your left foot at your right ankle. Pivoting on your right heel, bring your right palm near your ear (Fig. 63). Move your left hand and your left foot

74 · CHAPTER 4

65

66   67

backward in SNAKE step, turn to face front, and separate your arms,
your left palm deflecting high in CARRYING palm and your right palm
pushing forward, SUPPORTING, as in the T'ai-chi posture FAIR LADY
WORKS AT SHUTTLES. Your weight is 70% front-loaded (Fig. 64).
Finally, shift all your weight forward to your left leg and do SINGLE
CHANGE OF PALM as before, swinging out of it rightward, putting
your right foot down ahead, and walk, gradually turning your torso
and hands toward the center (Figs. 65, 66, 67).

68

69

70

6.   GIANT ROC SPREADS WINGS (*Ta P'eng Chan Ch'ih*)
Walking with your left hand toward the center (Fig. 68), toe-in your
right foot and turn your waist rightward, shifting your weight to your
right foot, your left forearm turning in across your body (Fig. 69). As
your waist begins to turn leftward, move your left arm in a clockwise
circle down, pivoting at the elbow (Fig. 70). Step to your left and forward with your left foot and circle your left hand, palm out and CUT-
TING upward, while retracting your right hand, palm up, to your right
hip (Fig. 71). Step forward with your right foot, toed-in, and make an
OX-TONGUE palm with your right hand at your right hip (Fig. 72).

76 · CHAPTER 4

71

72   73   74

75

76

77

78

Next, lift your left foot, toes down, knee high, as your left arm starts to sweep overhead (Fig. 73). Pivot to the left on your right heel and continue circling your left arm in GRASPING palm (Fig. 74) while you unclasp your right hook and circle it upward from the rear (Fig. 75). Now place your left foot down back on the circle in a 60% rear-weighted posture, simultaneously chopping with your right palm, and end by THRUSTING downward, slapping your palms en route. Your left palm protects the right side of your head—that side toward the center—and your right palm stops at waist level (Fig. 76).

As you shift your weight to your left foot, suspend your right foot at your left ankle and drop your left hand, palm up, on your right forearm, which has also been turned upward (Fig. 77). Step forward with your right foot and begin to walk (Fig. 78). As you walk, extend your crossed arms high and forward, separating them to each side in

WALKING THE CIRCLE · **79**

79

80

81

82

PHOENIX, walking style, your left STANDING palm, slightly higher than your right (Figs. 79–82). Figures 79–82 show arm movement from a static posture, to differentiate the arm movement for the reader. Actually, the arms only move—opening and extending—as you walk.

83

84

85

7. WHITE MONKEY PRESENTS A PEACH (*Pai Yuan Hsien T'ao*)

Walking with your left palm toward the center (Fig. 83), toe-in your
right foot deeply (Fig. 84). Turn your waist leftward, and, as it continues and your weight shifts onto your right foot, pivot your left foot
on its ball and open your arms (Fig. 85). Step forward with your left

86 87 88

89 90

foot to the circle (Fig. 86), and, as you shift your weight forward to it, raise your right leg, the knee high, and bring both palms upward as though carrying a tray with PIERCING palms (Fig. 87). Step out with your right foot and gradually turn your torso and hands toward the center as you walk (Figs. 88–90).

91   92   93

94   95   96

8. WHIRLWIND PALMS (*Hsuan Feng Chang*)

This change, which blends the palms, is also called EIGHT IMMOR-
TALS CROSS THE SEA (*Pa Hsien Kuo Hai*). Walking with your left
hand focused on the center (Fig. 91), toe-in your right foot in a wide
stance, dropping both arms as you turn your waist rightward (Fig. 92).
Step toward the center with your left foot, circling your left hand from
the elbow in a backhanded motion PIERCING downward, and retract
your right hand, palm up, in GRASPING palm, at your right hip (Figs.
93, 94). Toe-out your left foot, and, while pressing down your left
palm, step forward a full step with your right foot (Fig. 95). Put your
right foot down toed-in slightly, and, as your weight shifts onto your
right foot, turn your body sideward, your waist leading the action, and
PIERCE with your right palm over your depressing left SUPPORTING
palm (Fig. 96).

97 98

99 100

101 102

103

Now circle your left palm clockwise down and out to the side, palm up, but don't change your right palm (Fig. 97). Pivoting on your right heel, raise your left arm, palm down, over the right arm, which circles underneath, palm up (Fig. 98). Step back with your left foot in line with your right heel, into a HORSE stance, and shift your weight to it, turning your torso leftward while your arms remain in an "embrace" posture (Figs. 99, 100). As your weight begins to shift to your right foot, drop your hands, palms down, in a circle (Fig. 101). Continue shifting your weight to your right foot, taking your hands, palms in, upward in a counterclockwise circle (Fig. 102). Now shift your weight to your left foot and turn your waist leftward, carrying both CUTTING palms in, across your body (Fig. 103).

Still in the HORSE stance, and with most of your weight on your left foot, drop your left hand, palm up, near your right elbow and extend

104

105

106

107

108

your right hand forward, palm down (Fig. 104). Swing your right hand rightward, CUTTING laterally, your left palm following your right elbow, and your weight going to your right foot, your left foot suspended at your right ankle (Fig. 105).

Next, step forward, toeing out your left foot, and extend your right hand, GRASPING, palm out, overhead while PIERCING with your left hand, palm up, down and forward in the BALL-HOLDING posture (Fig. 106). Toe-in your right foot as you turn leftward, without changing your arms (Fig. 107). Shift your weight to your right foot while extending your right hand, palm up, to the side, circling your left hand, palm up, and suspending your left foot near your right knee (Fig. 108).

109   110   111

112   113

Pivoting on your right heel, bring your left arm over the descending right arm in an "embrace" posture, palms facing (Fig. 109). Completing the pivot on your right heel, put your left foot down in a 60% rear-weighted stance, CUTTING laterally with your left palm edge. Your right hand, palm up, follows your left elbow (Fig. 110). Do SINGLE CHANGE OF PALM and walk the circle with your right palm focused on the center (Figs. 111–113).

114

115

116

To close the exercise, walk with your right hand extended toward the center of circle. Toe-in your left foot (Fig. 114) and then toe-out your right foot until your feet are parallel, dropping your hands, your right on top, as you turn rightward (Fig. 115). Continue dropping your hands past your sides (Fig. 116) and bring them up and outward

117   118   119

120   121   122

overhead, palms down (Fig. 117). As you begin to press downward
(Fig. 118), turn your waist rightward (Fig. 119) and leftward (Fig.
120), then rightward and leftward once more, then back to the center
(Fig. 121) and stand (Fig. 122).

123

124

125

Alternatively, you may do Chen P'an-ling's shorter close. On the last step of walking with your right hand extended toward the center, bring your left (rear) foot up so that the heels almost touch, and then lower both hands, palms facing up below your navel, keeping both knees bent (Fig. 123). Raise both arms out to the sides and overhead, palms facing, and stand up and inhale (Fig. 124). Lower both hands, moving palms down the center of your body to your *tan-t'ien*. Bend you knees and exhale (Fig. 125).

5

Conclusion

The popularity of Pa-kua in China was greatly increased through the skill and the many publications of the famous Sun Lu-t'ang, whose *Ch'uan-i Shu Cheng* [The Real Explanation of Boxing (1929)] and *Pa-kua Ch'uan Hsueh* [A Study of Pa-kua Boxing (1916)] were written to present the true aspects of the art. We have used much of the information contained in his books in giving the introduction to the art and in talking about the Pa-kua masters. It is only natural, therefore, that we end this presentation of the art of Pa-kua with his own words.

The Tao permeates the universe and is the origin of both *yin* and *yang*. In boxing, the Tao is symbolized by the internal arts of Hsing-i, Pa-kua, and T'ai-chi. Although these three arts are different, they are based upon the same principle: everything begins, is, and ends in emptiness. One's original energy (*yuan ch'i*) must be maintained. This is the power that keeps the sky blue and that makes the earth calm; it is also the source of achievement in man. . . . Confucius said: "From the greatest sincerity comes the greatest achievement."

Diligent practice in the internal arts is, then, a discipline born out of sincerity, a system of self-control over conduct that leads to achievement. The word discipline itself comes from the Latin roots (*dis* + *capere*, to hold apart) meaning both a system of education and a method of training that employs rigorous control—thus, a leading forth of your true self through true self-control. Although fully Chinese in their conception and aesthetics, the three internal martial arts of Hsing-i, Pa-kua, and T'ai-chi are also excellent expressions of what the ancient Greeks called *aretē* (fr. Gr. *areskein*, to please; akin to *arariskein*, to fit), an ideal that embodies the concepts of excellence, valor, virtue, and manliness. Plato called it "the holistic striving for excellence in terms of beauty, strength, and wisdom." As in *aretē*, excellence in the internal arts is only possible while one is striving. Those who think that excellence has been attained and who slacken in their practice have already lost it. Thus, modest striving is required to achieve excellence, whereas overbearing pride will make the attainment of it impossible. Therefore, in your practice of Pa-kua, in order to best perfect your skills, always work hard and remain humble.

Finally, description is no substitute for practice. As Master Li Kuei-yuan once wrote: "Rules are taught by the teachers, but the essence can only be comprehended by the boxer himself." And the essence can only be obtained through practice. Put simply, as you practice you obtain the essence.

Index

K'an Ling-feng, 23
Ken, 19
Ku Chi-tzu, 20
kua, 16, 53
Kuo Feng-ch'ih, 6, 27, 50
Kuo Yun-shen, 20
K'an, 19
K'an Ling-feng, 23
k'ou, 41
K'un, 18

Lao-tzu, 39
li, 18, 40, 41
Li Han-chang, 23
Li Kuei-yuan, 94
Li Ts'un-i, 23
Li Wen-piao, 23
Liang Chen-pu, 23
Little Nine-Heaven Boxing, 47
Liu Feng-ch'un, 22, 23
liver, 18
lo, 51
"Lotus-leaf Palm," 41, 56
lungs, 19

Ma (disciple of Chang Chao-tung), 24
Ma Wei-chi, 22, 23, 24
Manchu government, 21–22
mind, as the source of all action, 30
Mount Omei, 20, 24
muscular training, as eschewed by internal styles, 28
Mysterious Gate Boxing, 49

natural feelings, importance of, 20

naturalness, 33
nei-chia, 15
"*Nei-kuo, wai ch'eng,* 42; see also "Internally bound, externally stretched"
Nine Palaces. *See* Nine Stations
Nine Stations, 47–48, 55
Niu Liang-ch'en, 20
nothing (*wu-wei*), as the only thing the student must do, 29–30

original energy, 93
overturn, 51
OX-TONGUE PALM, 57, 76

Pa Hsien Kuo Hai, 83
pact, requiring all Hsing-i and Pa-kua students to cross train, 20
Pai She T'u Shen, 72
Pai Yuan Hsien T'ao, 81
Pa-kua: basic three axioms of, 31; as circular, 30, 39; compared with Hsing-i and T'ai-chi, 30; definition of, 15; as difficult, 40; as having emerged from the hidden Taoist ranks, 22; essence of, 18, 53, 94; and Hsing-i, as complementary, 20; main principles of, 39–42; masters of, 19–27; as never to be used, 39; origin of, as unknown, 19; philosophy and practice of, 15–19; popularity of, in China, 93; as requiring twenty years to master, 31; and Sun Lu-t'ang, 93; transmission of force in, 56; Wang Shu-chin's method of, 24–26, 61

Other Titles in the Tuttle Library of Martial Arts

AIKIDO AND THE DYNAMIC SPHERE
by Adele Westbrook and Oscar Ratti

Aikido is a Japanese method of self-defense that can be used against any form of attack and that is also a way of harmonizing all of one's vital powers into an integrated, energy-filled whole.

BLACK BELT KARATE *by Jordan Roth*

A no-frills, no-holds barred handbook on the fundamentals of modern karate. Over 800 techniques and exercises and more than 1,850 photographs reveal the speed and power inherent in properly taught karate.

THE ESSENCE OF OKINAWAN KARATE-DO
by Shoshin Nagamine

"Nagamine's book will awaken in all who read it a new understanding of the Okinawan open-handed martial art."

—Gordon Warner
Kendo 7th dan. renshi

THE HAND IS MY SWORD: A KARATE HANDBOOK *by Robert A. Trias*

The history, the fundamentals, and the basic techniques and katas are brought to life by over 600 illustrations in this book, which teaches that to master others one must first master oneself.

JUDO FORMAL TECHNIQUES *by Tadao Otaki and Donn F. Draeger*

A comprehensive manual on the basic formal techniques of Kodokan Judo, the Randori no Kata, which provide the fundamental training in throwing and grappling that is essential to effective Judo.

KOREAN KARATE: FREE-FIGHTING TECHNIQUES *by Sihak Henry Cho*

This book teaches Tae-Kwon Do, probably the strongest form of self-defense known. This Korean form of karate is highly competitive, and its practice is one of the best ways to achieve mental and physical fitness.

THE NINJA AND THEIR SECRET FIGHTING ART *by Stephen K. Hayes*

The *ninja* were the elusive spies and assassins of feudal Japan. This book explains their lethal system of unarmed combat, unique weapons, and mysterious techniques of stealth.

PRACTICAL KARATE Series *by M. Nakayama and Donn F. Draeger*

Book I   Fundamentals
Book II   Against the Unarmed Assailant
Book III Against Multiple Unarmed Assailants
Book IV   Against Armed Assailants
Book V   For Women
Book VI   In Special Situations

STICKFIGHTING: A PRACTICAL GUIDE TO SELF-PROTECTION *by Evan S. Baltazzi*

Over 400 photographs illustrate in a systematic way the simple, versatile, and comprehensive approach to a method of self-protection accessible to all.

T'AI-CHI: THE "SUPREME ULTIMATE" EXERCISE *by Cheng Man-ch'ing and Robert W. Smith*

Written by one of the leading Yang-style experts, who studied directly under the legendary Yang Cheng-fu (d. 1935), this book illustrates Cheng's famous short form and includes a translation of the *T'ai-chi Ch'uan Classics*.

THE TECHNIQUES OF JUDO *by Shinzo Takagaki and Harold E. Sharp*

A fully illustrated and authoritative manual giving step-by-step explanations, practical pointers, and thorough analyses of all of the most commonly used *waza* of judo.

THIS IS KENDO *by Junzo Sasamori and Gordon Warner*

The first book in English to describe the origin and history of kendo, its basic principles and techniques, its etiquette, and its relation to Zen. A must for any serious martial artist.

THE WAY OF KARATE *by George E. Mattson*

A fully illustrated explanation of the Okinawan style of karate; an indispensable introduction to its true nature and basic techniques, with emphasis on its value in both training and self-defense.

Another exciting title in Tuttle's
Chinese Martial Arts Library
Hsing-i: Chinese Internal Boxing
by Robert W. Smith and Allen Pittman

Hsing-i is one of the most complete systems of self-defense ever developed. This new book, by the world's leading authority on Chinese boxing, gives a thorough account of the history and philosophy behind the art; it also introduces to the West the orthodox style of the late master Ch'en P'an-ling.

The authors describe in great detail, using over 260 photographs, the basic techniques, the five fists, a linked form of the five fists, and the twelve animal styles. Using this easy-to-follow text, any student can probe deeply into the hitherto hidden secrets of Hsing-i.

Robert W. Smith is famous for his pioneering work in introducing the Chinese martial arts to the West; many of his texts are classics in the field. **Allen Pittman,** Smith's senior student, collaborated on this book after several years of full-time study and research in Taiwan.